W9-BZB-234

Jun'22 51010

COUNTRY PROFILES

MEXICO

BY MARTY GITLIN

BLASTOFF!
DISCOVERY

BELLWETHER MEDIA • MINNEAPOLIS, MN

Blastoff! Discovery launches
a new mission: reading to learn.
Filled with facts and features, each
book offers you an exciting new
world to explore!

This edition first published in 2018 by Bellwether Media, Inc.

No part of this publication may be reproduced in whole or in
part without written permission of the publisher.
For information regarding permission, write to Bellwether
Media, Inc., Attention: Permissions Department,
5357 Penn Avenue South, Minneapolis, MN 55419.

Library of Congress Cataloging-in-Publication Data

Names: Gitlin, Marty, author.
Title: Mexico / by Marty Gitlin.
Description: Minneapolis, MN : Bellwether Media, Inc.,
    [2018.] | Series: Blastoff! Discovery: Country Profiles |
    Includes bibliographical references and index. | Audience:
    Grades 3-8. | Audience: Ages 7-13.
Identifiers: LCCN 2016058971 (print) | LCCN 2016059897
    (ebook) | ISBN 9781626176850 (hardcover : alk. paper) |
    ISBN 9781681034157 (ebook)
Subjects: LCSH: Mexico–Juvenile literature.
Classification: LCC F1208.5 .G57 2018 (print) | LCC F1208.5
    (ebook) | DDC 972–dc23
LC record available at https://lccn.loc.gov/2016058971

Editor: Christina Leaf   Designer: Brittany McIntosh

Printed in the United States of America, North Mankato, MN.

TABLE OF CONTENTS

EL CASTILLO
CHICHÉN ITZÁ

Tourists arrive in the ancient Mexican city of Chichén Itzá. Soon, the pyramid of El Castillo comes into view. The guests imagine climbing the 79-foot (24-meter) temple a thousand years ago. That is when historians believe it was built by the Mayan Indians.

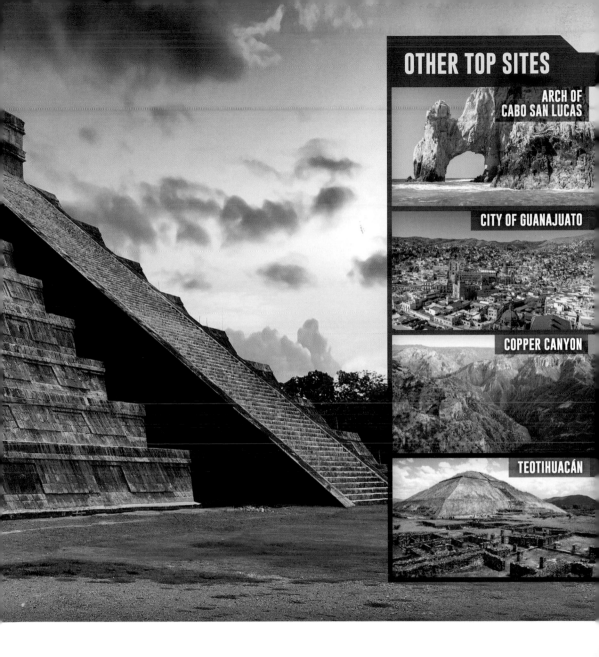

OTHER TOP SITES

ARCH OF CABO SAN LUCAS

CITY OF GUANAJUATO

COPPER CANYON

TEOTIHUACÁN

The tourists have arrived on a special day, the spring **equinox**. They wait for the sun to set. As it sinks lower, the light and shadows look like a snake crawling down the stairway. Legend says that this wonder was how the Mayans honored the god Kukulkan, a feathered **serpent**. It is one of the many marvels of Mexico!

5

Mexico is a North American country that shares its northern border with the United States. Its east coast sits on the shores of the **Gulf** of Mexico. Belize and Guatemala are located to the south. To its west are the Pacific Ocean and the Gulf of California. The gulf separates Mexico's Baja California **peninsula** from the rest of the country.

Mexico covers 758,449 square miles (1,964,375 square kilometers). Its capital is Mexico City, which rests in the south-central part of the country.

TIJUANA

BAJA CALIFORNIA

GULF OF CALIFORNIA

PACIFIC OCEAN

N
W + E
S

UNITED STATES

MONTERREY

MEXICO

GULF OF MEXICO

PUEBLA

GUADALAJARA

MEXICO CITY

BELIZE

GUATEMALA

Deserts dominate the northern regions of Mexico. The Rio Grande river runs along the northern border. Running north to south through long strips of the country are the Sierra Madre mountains. The grasslands of the Mexican **Plateau** sit in between the mountainous areas. **Tropical** forests provide **habitats** for animals in the south.

RIO GRANDE

N
W+E
S

◻ = SIERRA MADRE MOUNTAINS

RIO GRANDE
MEXICAN BORDER

SUMIDERO CANYON
NATIONAL PARK
CHIAPAS

MEXICO CITY
**Average
seasonal highs
and lows**

JANUARY
HIGH: 70 °F (21 °C)
LOW: 41 °F (5 °C)

APRIL
HIGH: 77 °F (25 °C)
LOW: 50 °F (10 °C)

JULY
HIGH: 72 °F (22 °C)
LOW: 54 °F (12 °C)

OCTOBER
HIGH: 73 °F (23 °C)
LOW: 50 °F (10 °C)

°F = degrees Fahrenheit
°C = degrees Celsius

The tropical location of southern Mexico results in little temperature change there. Northern Mexico experiences scorching heat in summer but cold temperatures each winter. Rainfall is rare in most areas throughout the year. Hurricanes threaten the low-lying coastal areas from August to October.

Mexico's variety of habitats shelter many types of animals. Rattlesnakes and poisonous lizards lurk in the deserts. Nine-banded armadillos try to roll themselves into balls for protection from predators.

Fast, powerful jaguars hunt monkeys and pig-like tapirs in coastal **rain forests**. In winter, forests fill with birds that have **migrated** from the northern countries to escape the chill. Nearly one billion monarch butterflies also flutter from Canada to the central highlands of Mexico each year.

JAGUAR

RATTLESNAKE

NINE-BANDED ARMADILLO

CACTUS CENTRAL

Mexico is a cactus capital! The tallest cactus species in the world is the *cardón*, in the Sonoran Desert. It measures nearly 66 feet (20 meters) tall.

BLACK
HOWLER MONKEY

BLACK
HOWLER MONKEY

Life Span: 20 years
Red List Status: endangered

black howler monkey range = ▪

LEAST CONCERN	NEAR THREATENED	VULNERABLE	ENDANGERED	CRITICALLY ENDANGERED	EXTINCT IN THE WILD	EXTINCT
			▲			

The more than 123 million people that live in Mexico are called Mexicans. About two of every three are of mixed **native** and European descent. They are known as *mestizos*. Many others are of native **heritage**.

Nearly all Mexicans speak Spanish. The native language of Nahuatl has about 1.5 million speakers. The Aztec people spoke this language centuries ago. Most Mexicans are Roman Catholic. No other religion has a major following in Mexico.

FAMOUS FACE

Name: Diego Luna
Birthday: December 29, 1979
Hometown: Mexico City, Mexico
Famous for: An actor in many movies, including *Rogue One: A Star Wars Story*, in which he played Cassian Andor

MEXICO CITY

SPEAK SPANISH

ENGLISH	SPANISH	HOW TO SAY IT
hello	hola	OH-lah
goodbye	adiós	ah-dee-OHS
please	por favor	pohr fah-VOR
thank you	gracias	grah-SEE-ahs
yes	sí	SEE
no	no	noh

COMMUNITIES

TAXCO

Family is very important to Mexicans. Mexican families have gotten smaller over the years. However, in **rural** areas they may be larger. Recent **immigration** has begun to separate Mexican families. Members may move to the United States so they can send money back home.

Nearly four in five Mexicans live in **urban** areas. They often live in small, boxy apartments. **Traditional** Spanish-style stone houses remain common in older areas of Mexico City. Mud brick homes are scattered throughout the countryside. Many Mexicans have cars. However, heavy traffic in Mexico City has motivated a growing trend of bicycle riding.

EARNING THOSE CAR KEYS

For many years, Mexico City motorists did not need to pass a driving test for their license. The result was thousands of accidents. In 2014, the law changed to require a passed driving test.

MEXICO CITY

CUSTOMS

Mexicans are traditionally warm-natured. They welcome unexpected visitors into their homes. Social gatherings such as dinner parties are followed by spirited conversations well into the night. It is considered rude to leave right after dinner.

The **plaza** serves as a social center for many Mexicans. Plazas are found in small villages and large cities. People meet there to talk and listen to music. They also gather to buy and sell clothes, food, and other goods in the marketplace. Farmers might trade goods rather than sell them. The result is lively **bartering**.

MARKETPLACE

PLAZA DE ARMAS
GUADALAJARA

TV CLASS

Many rural students in Mexico learn through classes on television called *Telesecundaria*. The program began in 1968 to improve secondary education.

School in Mexico is required between the ages of 6 to 18. Children must also attend one year of preschool. Rural schools have trouble attracting good teachers. They often lack the money to run properly. Some families cannot afford school fees. This means many children struggle to get a good education. But each year more and more children are going to school.

Service jobs employ more than half of all Mexicans. They work in government offices, banks, and stores. Other workers produce goods such as iron, steel, clothing, and cars. Crops produced by Mexican farmers include mangoes and avocados.

FABRIC SHOP WORKER

AVOCADO FARMER

BULLFIGHTING

Mexicans love soccer! Millions watch and play the game. Bullfighting events are also attended by huge crowds in stadiums. People enjoy such sports as baseball and basketball as well.

SOCCER

Different parts of Mexico feature sports unique to the region. Coastal areas attract swimmers and surfers. At La Quebrada, brave divers plunge 136 feet (41 meters) from cliffs into the Pacific Ocean. Hikers climb peaks in Mexico's mountains. Horseback riders enjoy the trails in northern ranch regions.

LUCHA LIBRE

One popular spectator activity is *lucha libre*. In this dramatic style of professional wrestling, competitors act out roles of good and evil. The winners of the matches are often determined before they take place.

LA GALLINITA CIEGA

La Gallinita Ciega is called "The Little Blind Hen" in English.

How to Play:
1. Blindfold one player to be the "little blind hen."

2. Spin the "hen" around.

3. The "hen" must find and tag another player. The other players give hints about their locations by talking or squawking like chickens.

4. The game continues until all the players are tagged. Then a new "hen" is chosen.

YUMMY...*CACTUS?*

Mexicans eat *nopales*, or cactus stems, as a vegetable. These often come from prickly pear cacti.

The corn tortilla is a **staple** of the Mexican diet. Various fillings in tortillas create such popular foods as quesadillas, enchiladas, and tacos. Mexicans also enjoy meat, fish, or vegetables combined with rice. Squash is a common vegetable. A mid-afternoon lunch is the biggest meal of the day in Mexico. Mexicans enjoy a light dinner late in the evening.

Favorite foods in Mexico include a seafood dish called *ceviche*. A pork and cornmeal soup called *pozole* is also popular. Around Independence Day, people enjoy *chiles en nogada*, meat-stuffed chili peppers in a cream sauce. Some people in Mexico eat fried grasshoppers!

CEVICHE

CHILES EN NOGADA

HORCHATA RECIPE

Ingredients:

1 cup long-grain white rice

1-2 cinnamon sticks
(or 1 tablespoon ground cinnamon)

5 cups water

1/4 cup sweetened condensed milk

1/4 teaspoon vanilla extract

Steps:

1. Soak the rice and cinnamon sticks in 4 cups of hot (not boiling) water for at least 4 hours. If using ground cinnamon, wait to add in step 4.

2. After it is done soaking, have an adult help you blend the mixture in a blender until smooth.

3. Using a cheesecloth, strain liquid out of the mixture into a large bowl. Throw away whatever mixture is left over. Save the liquid.

4. Add condensed milk, vanilla extract, and 1 cup of water to the strained liquid. Stir to combine.

5. Serve with ice and a sprinkle of ground cinnamon!

DÍA DE LOS
MUERTOS

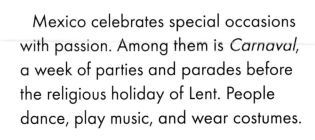

Mexico celebrates special occasions with passion. Among them is *Carnaval*, a week of parties and parades before the religious holiday of Lent. People dance, play music, and wear costumes.

Mexicans mark Independence Day on September 16. Celebrations begin the night before with a battle cry called *El Grito*. Native heritage is honored during *Día de la Raza* on October 12. Mexicans honor the dead during *Día de los Muertos*. It is believed that on November 2, the spirits of the dead visit their loved ones. Every event gives Mexicans a chance to show how proud they are of their country!

GIVING PETS A LITTLE RELIGION

One fun holiday is Saint Anthony's Day on January 17. That is when Mexicans can take their pets to church for a blessing.

1521
Spaniards conquer the
Aztecs and start a colony

1862
Battle of Puebla marks
a victory over the
French, launching the
Cinco de Mayo holiday

250
Mayan culture begins
to reach a peak

1917
Following the 1910
Revolution, a new
constitution is approved

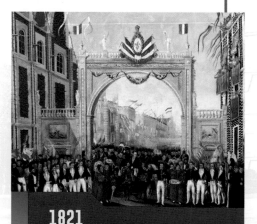

1848
Mexico gives up territory
to the U.S. after their
defeat in war, including
present-day Nevada,
Utah, California, and parts
of Wyoming, Colorado,
Arizona, and New Mexico

1821
Mexico gains
independence from Spain

1985
Deadly earthquake strikes Mexico City

1953
Women gain right to vote

1990
Octavio Paz is celebrated as the first Mexican to win the Nobel Prize in Literature

2016
Famous criminal Joaquín "El Chapo" Guzmán is caught

1968
Mexico hosts the Summer Olympics

Official Name: United Mexican States

Flag of Mexico: The Mexican flag features green, white, and red vertical stripes. The green stripe represents independence from Spain. The white stripe symbolizes the Catholic faith. The red stripe honors bravery. In the middle is Mexico's coat of arms. It shows an eagle on a cactus with a snake in its beak. According to legend, an Aztec leader was told in a dream that he would see this image. He was directed to build a city there. The city became Tenochtitlan, which later became Mexico City.

Area: 758,449 square miles
(1,964,375 square kilometers)

Capital City: Mexico City

Important Cities: Guadalajara, Puebla, Tijuana, Monterrey, León

Population:
123,166,749 (July 2016)

WHERE PEOPLE LIVE

COUNTRYSIDE
20.8%

CITY
79.2%

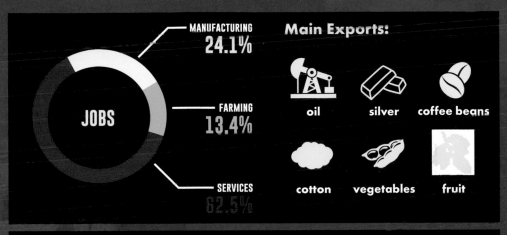

MANUFACTURING
24.1%

JOBS

FARMING
13.4%

SERVICES
62.5%

Main Exports:

oil   silver   coffee beans

cotton   vegetables   fruit

National Holiday:
Independence Day (September 16)

Main Language:
Spanish

Form of Government:
federal presidential republic

Title for Country Leader:
president

JEHOVAH'S WITNESS
1.4%

OTHER

RELIGION

NONE
4.7%

CHRISTIAN
84.3%

Unit of Money:
Mexican *peso*

GLOSSARY

bartering—trading by exchanging goods rather than using money

equinox—the time in the spring and fall when the sun crosses the equator, making night and day the same length all over the earth

gulf—part of an ocean or sea that extends into land

habitats—lands with certain types of plants, animals, and weather

heritage—the background or history of a group of people

immigration—the act of moving from one country to another

migrated—traveled from one place to another, often with the seasons

native—originally from the area or related to a group of people that began in the area

peninsula—a section of land that extends out from a larger piece of land and is almost completely surrounded by water

plateau—an area of flat, raised land

plaza—a public square in a city or town

rain forests—thick, green forests that receive a lot of rain

rural—related to the countryside

serpent—a large snake

service jobs—jobs that perform tasks for people or businesses

staple—a widely used food or other item

tourists—people who travel to visit another place

traditional—related to customs, ideas, or beliefs handed down from one generation to the next

tropical—part of the tropics; the tropics is a hot, rainy region near the equator.

urban—related to cities and city life

TO LEARN MORE

AT THE LIBRARY

Honders, Christine. *Ancient Maya Culture*. New York, N.Y.: PowerKids Press, 2017.

Kent, Deborah. *Mexico*. New York, N.Y.: Children's Press, 2012.

Peppas, Lynn. *Cultural Traditions in Mexico*. New York, N.Y.: Crabtree Pub. Co., 2012.

ON THE WEB

Learning more about Mexico is as easy as 1, 2, 3.

1. Go to www.factsurfer.com.

2. Enter "Mexico" into the search box.

3. Click the "Surf" button and you will see a list of related web sites.

With factsurfer.com, finding more information is just a click away.

INDEX